Comings and Goings

Poetry by Tova Milinsky

*"Nothing is more important in life than
'Comings and Goings.'"*
~Margaret Weiner, A.C.S.W.

WISDOM PRESS

Comings and Goings

Copyright © 2013 by Tova Milinsky

Layout and cover design by Jacqueline L. Challiss Hill
Cover photo by Ariel Milinsky
Printed in the United States of America

Summary: A collection of poems by Tova Milinsky.

Library of Congress Cataloging-in-Publication Data
  Milinsky, Tova
  Comings and Goings/Tova Milinsky–Second Edition
  ISBN-13: 978-1-938326-22-6
  1. Poetry. 2. Literary collections.
  I. Milinsky, Tova II. Title
  Library of Congress Control Number: 2013945822

WISDOM PRESS

Wisdom Press is an imprint of Nelson Publishing & Marketing
366 Welch Road, Northville, MI 48167
www.nelsonpublishingandmarketing.com
(248) 735-0418

Comings and Goings

"Comings" and "Goings" are landmarks of life,
They illustrate time that we've spent
On the roadway we've traveled from Birth until Death,
Shaped and molded by change and event.

We arrive on the scene through no plan of our own,
But this act becomes ours when it's done,
As the first venture out on our personal path,
It's no doubt a significant one.

There's no turning back as the road stretches out,
And the road, long and narrow, may bend.
Wherever we've journeyed, on high road or low,
We're a Traveler until the road ends.

Contents

Copyright
Comings and Goings
Contents
Acknowledgments
Foreword by Beth Hedva

Beginnings

Life Encounters and Transitions

*"Insomnia" was originally published in *Iambs & Trochees*, Journal III, Issue 1, Spring 2004, page 59. Permission granted by Joseph S. Salemi to republish.

Reflection and Wisdom

*"Sounds of Silence" was originally published in *Hidden Oak Poetry Journal*, Spring, 2004, page 56.

Acknowledgments

This book is presented as a type of emotional roadmap of the stages in one's journey through life. These stages are highlighted in the introductory quatrains preceding each section, while the ensuing poems are selected illustrations of these "developmental" encounters.

At this time I especially wish to thank Beth Hedva and Harold Finkleman for their efforts in conceiving and executing the original publishing project, which became an intercontinental achievement before it was done.

In addition I want to thank Marilyn McGrath, whose talented and accepting instruction helped forge the Arizona Writers Group from those of us with diverse backgrounds and perspectives into a "family" with deep bonds and sincere admiration for each other's achievements.

Within this group, my special thanks go to Ann Graff,

who was always ready to transcribe the poems and type them to mail to publishers for possible submissions, and joined my endeavors with wholehearted enthusiasm and love.

Special thanks to spoken word poet Sheri-D Wilson, a very recent recipient of the CBC award designating her as one of the "Top 10 Canadian Poets." She read, critiqued, offered suggestions and encouragement to me to pursue publication of my poems.

Also important is to recognize the quote "Nothing is more important in life than 'Comings and Goings,'" and its myriad implications, by Margaret Weiner, MSW, my friend and supervisor at the Jewish Family and Children Services Agency in Detroit, Michigan.

Most of all I want to thank my other children, Debby Milinsky and Assad Sobky; Sharon Milinsky and Jeffrey Axelrod and Joel and Yvonne Milinsky. Special thanks to Yvonne and Ariel Milinsky for illustrations and Ariel's digital-magic-photography that are within this manuscript. I want to include all my five grandchildren, Vanessa and Travis Wright, Jamie and Sara Axelrod, and Ariel Milinsky for all their wonderful love and support.

Again, many thanks for the love and support of extended family and friends over the years.

Foreword

By Beth Hedva

This compilation of Tova Milinsky's work was originally planned as a special edition for friends, colleagues, writing partners, family, children, grandchildren—those of us who felt we had been touched by her life most closely—and of course those who have been touched by her as a social worker, community worker, and artist. The effort drew significant creative attention. *Comings and Goings* shares wisdom gleaned over her lifetime of "comings and goings." We appreciate the professional input and reflections her poetry has attracted and the assistance and artistic contributions of her daughter-in-law Yvonne Milinsky and her granddaughter Ariel Milinsky.

Tova Milinsky's poems are reflections of life. From the fun and subtle to disturbing social commentary; from free-verse with no rhyme to humorous and well-crafted villanelles—a highly structured French poetic form, like "Villanelle: 'Sleepless Night'"—they all contain sparks of a keen intelligence that leads to personal insight and awareness. Tova has been a sounding board, mirror, and reflector of deeper insight and wisdom. Her poems will continue to do this; and I imagine her poetry will allow us to share her wit and wisdom with each other and many others for generations to come.

Beginnings

Beginnings are hard and
Put you on the spot.
Sometimes they're easy,
But mostly they're not.

Creation: A Poem

In the beginning
It grew from the top down.
Intellectually, with
Words,
Phrases,
Metaphors, and
Rhythm.
Suddenly, it rose from the inside.
Thrusting forward,
Forceful,
Impelling, and
Bursting to breathe free!

Villanelle: "Poetease"

I'll try to write a villanelle,
A poem with an easy rhyme.
It's very simple I've heard tell.

The meter's rhythm rose and fell,
Inviting me to count the time.
I'll try to write a villanelle.

Insistent sounds I cannot quell,
To fail at this would be a crime.
It's very simple I've heard tell.

There are no words to break the spell,
For this there is no paradigm.
I'll try to write a villanelle.

The meter's rhythm will foretell,
If I'm a poet or a mime.
It's very simple I've heard tell.

If I could rhyme all would be well,
Ignore the meter so sublime.
I'll try to write a villanelle.
It's very simple I've heard tell.

"How It Began" Circa 1945

"Reduce in Lady Esther's care!"
"For upset stomachs—One-a-Day!"
"You'll find it none the worse for wear!"
"Duz does your clothes without delay!"

"For upset stomachs—One-a-Day!"
"Yes! Pepsi-Cola hits the spot!"
"Duz does your clothes without delay!"
"Insured for stains—the Rytex pot!"

"Yes, Pepsi-Cola hits the spot!"
"This daring shade, a fashion must!"
"Insured for stains—the Rytex pot!"
"For cakes and pies use Flakey Crust!"

"This daring shade, a fashion must!"
"The beer that always keeps its head!"
"For cakes and pies use Flakey Crust!"
"Why don't you smoke Pall Malls instead?"

"The beer that always keeps its head!"
(It's good to know that someone can.)
"Why don't you smoke Pall Malls instead?"
This was the new commercial plan.

It's good to know that someone can.
Reduce in Lady Esther's care.
This was the new commercial plan.
You'll find it none the worse for wear!

Around the Clock with Baby

At six a.m. the baby cries.
You rub the slumber from your eyes
You stumble out and in your daze,
Two solemn eyes return your gaze.
The next decision's up to you,
To nurse or bottle-feed, it's true.
In either instance, it is clear
You always hold the baby near.
And now the infant at your breast
Has gone to sleep and you can rest.

At ten a.m. what do you hear?
A voice that's music to your ear!
But maybe now's the time for fun—
A time to bathe the little one.
The water's warm and such a joy,
For every slippery girl or boy.
And when the baby's dry and fed,
You'll put it right back into bed.

It's two p.m. what do you know?
It's luncheon time for baby—so,
Assemble cereal and spoon.
Did six weeks really go so soon?
And soon the infant at your breast
Is fast asleep and you can rest.

It's four o'clock. This can't be beat!
It's not the time to nap or eat.
Now, what to do for girl or boy?
A little water? Or a toy?
And just because it is so dear,
It's fun to hold the baby near.

It's six p.m. The table's set,
Some relaxation you will get.
A chance to listen to the news,
Or to exchange some adult views.

But, Hark! What was that sound you heard?
It can't be baby! That's absurd!
Or is it? Yes, the time is here.
It's dinner time for baby dear.
Then place the baby in its bed,
Now maybe Mom and Dad get fed.

The clock has finished striking ten.
It's time to feed the kid again.
But as you enter baby's room,
The crying stops and all the gloom
Just disappears. Your step is known.
Your voice is heard. You're not alone.

There is a person in that bed,
Who's yours until the day it's wed.
But not to own—to love and share,
The joys and sorrows of its care.
And just because it feels so dear,
You want to hold it very near.

It's two a.m. hard to believe!
You try your good dream to retrieve.
One thing you know this just can't last,
And you'll be happy when it's passed.
And you'll recall the life you led,
When keeping baby dry and fed.

Villanelle: "Sleepless Night"

She went to bed to sleep.
Her blankets on her feet.
She started counting sheep.

She felt the hours creep.
She tangled with the sheet.
She went to bed to sleep.

Soon dawn began to peep.
The room had too much heat.
She kept on counting sheep.

She felt that she could weep.
Her mood was none too sweet.
She went to bed to sleep.

Her blankets in a heap.
To dream would be a treat.
She kept on counting sheep.

She almost thought she'd leap
From window ledge to street.
She went to bed to sleep.
She hated all those sheep.

Education

And is it true that when it rains
It's just the angels wringing out their clothes?
Or when they shake their pillows out
And let the feathers fly, we say it snows?
If that is so, then what is hail?
And how can thunder be explained away?

Child, that is something else. Besides,
I've used up all my answers for today.

School Daze

You learn about rules on the first day of school
After leaving the safety of home.
The teacher is kind but expects you to mind
Her directions to sit and not roam.
The children are new, they don't know about you,
And you cannot remember their names.
In a circle you walk and you try not to talk
While the teacher is teaching new games.

Pretty soon school is done and you sort of had fun
Even though things were scary and new.
And you realize tomorrow (with both pride and sorrow)
There's a seat in that school room for you!

Challenges

It rained and I stepped carefully around
The puddles scattered on the ground.
And I recalled the times long gone
When puddles were challenges.

The boys would pause at puddles' edge
To briefly gauge the depth, I guess.
Then forcefully stomp the mid-most spot.
The winners' water splashed the most.

The girls would try to jump the width.
And you could nearly always tell
By muddy droplets on the backs
Of socks and legs if they had made it.

Who says there are no differences?

Company

When the Muse comes
And sits inside your head,
You may be extremely tired
But you leave your cozy bed
And you write.

When the Muse comes
And occupies your brain,
Though you may appear attentive
On the inside you're in pain
Over the rhyme scheme.

When the Muse comes
And lodges in your chest,
You may long for some cessation
But the writer cannot rest
Words keep coming.

When the Muse comes
And visits in your heart,
There's a wave of satisfaction
When, at last, it does depart
And you're finished.

Choosing:
Ballade of Gentlemen's Names

Barnaby, son of exhortation.
Aaron, the lofty mountaineer.
Caesar defies abbreviation.
Richard the Lion knows no fear.
Epaminondas sounds sincere.
Every name has a certain shine,
Yet if I had to choose from here,
None would I ever choose for mine.

John (his parents used modulation).
Oliver somehow seems austere.
Samson glories in exultation,
And Percival must persevere.
Claudius frowns with stiff veneer.
Bacchus, jubilant god of wine.
Though each one must have something dear,
None would I ever choose for mine.

Not that I lack appreciation.
Not that I wish to sound severe.
But none of them holds the fascination
That does the one name I revere.
The name that's music to my ear.
So though these names are good and fine
(I lift my voice…perhaps HE'LL hear),
None would I ever choose for mine.

Paul is promised a bright career.
Matthias means "a gift divine."
Charlie enlivens the atmosphere.
But…DANNY'S the one I would choose for mine!

Blind Date

My father had a colleague,
A writer and a friend.
They'd sit and talk together
For hours without end.

This colleague had an offspring,
His only son and heir.
He mentioned to my father
We'd make a charming pair.

My father thought it over
And figured it'd be nice.
The dads arranged an outing
To help us break the ice.

The son called to confirm this
And I agreed to meet.
My wish was for Prince Charming,
My thoughts were pure and sweet.

I was fifteen and bashful,
Straight-laced and rather prim.
The boys I knew were likewise
And thus I pictured him.

He came and rang the doorbell,
I opened up the door.
In one revealing moment,
I saw what was in store.

He was head to toe a vision
In style of great repute.
Dressed in the latest fashion,
Adorned in a zoot suit.

His shoulders wide and ranging,
Then tapering to the hips.
The trousers full and baggy,
Pegged cuffs the size of ships.

A chain hung down the pant leg.
He twirled it once or twice.
His hat, broad-brimmed and pointy,
He thought he looked quite nice.

From there the date went downward.
He tried hard to impress.
He bragged about his prowess
In sports, in school, in chess.

He was, no doubt, a wizard
In math of any sort.
I felt his expectations
Of me fell far too short.

The movie was a failure.
His moves were well-defined.
No doubt he'd had some coaching,
He didn't think I'd mind.

The arm around the shoulder,
The hand upon the knee.
Whoever he thought he was out with
It surely wasn't me!

The bus ride home was quiet
With nothing left to say.
Some filial disobedience
Would sure have saved my day.

At last upon the doorstep
I offered him my hand.
He roughly grabbed and kissed me,
An action he had planned.

Once safe inside I realized
That what I most abhorred,
Was my feeling our whole evening
Was to see how well he scored.

Some good came from that meeting.
Before some time had passed,
I figured such adventures
Would be my first and last.

The years change one's perspective
And mellow out the view.
No doubt it was his first date,
He didn't know what to do.

Whoever was his mentor
Forgot what all aver:
"Omit technique and trappings
And concentrate on HER!"

The New One

The babe was in his cradle,
The mother sat close by.
The older children hopeful
He'd soon begin to cry.
No doubt if he was naughty
He wouldn't last too long.
She'd send him back forever.
She'd know he was all wrong.

The group sat in a circle
In all their usual chairs.
Their comfort zone was fractured
When they cast their furtive stares.
One empty chair was present
(Their reason for distress).
It signified "the New One"
With no means of redress.

The daughter brought her boyfriend.
She wished to make it known,
To all her friends and loved ones,
He soon would be her own.
The family's calm was shattered,
Could they believe their ears?
Who was this upstart stranger?
They smiled to hide their fears.

Such is "the New One's" fortune,
True welcome not his lot.
He'll have to learn the hard way,
He has to earn his spot.
And each successive entry
No matter, lose or win,
Repeats the birth-time trauma
For those "outside" or "in."

On Getting "In"

"In" is the place.
If you're "in"
It's your space.

If you're "out"
You've lost face.

When you're "in"
"You're okay"
And it's always
Your day.
To be "in"
Is to win,
And your face
Wears a grin!

All the world
Is your kin
When you're "in"!

Life Encounters and Transitions

Changes come often
(Not quite every day.)
It pays to expect them
As we go on our way.

Packing

Packing is lacking
In mountains of fun.
I cringe to consider
The ordeal begun.
Decisions are endless
Conclusions are few.
Projections for unknowns
Foolhardy to do.

The first cross is climate,
The second is size.
What looks good at outset
Results in surprise.
While too long a time
Spent in rain or in cold,
Ends up in disaster
As options grow old.

And then there are wrinkles,
The bane of the shift
Of pressure and handling
Too rough or too swift.
Restrictions from airlines
My choice countermands.
Dimensions of luggage
Impinge on the plans.
Some souls pack in leisure
"Keep the wolf from the door."
While some avoid panic
Till hours before.

Coda:
However I manage
This challenging chore
The process of packing
Is hardly a bore.

9/11

And it was evening.
And it was morning.

And the world awoke.
And the world **A W O K E!**
And the world

a

   w

     o

       k

         e.

Never to sleep the same.
Nor dream the same.

And the world shuddered.
And the world wept.
And the world grieved.

Lament to...

Ah! Love! But to find and
Now to lose you!
Would that I might have a
Second chance.
Have you found another to
Amuse you?
Is that why you've broken
Our romance?

Is it some deed or word
I spoke
That turned you from me
In this way?
From my embittered dreams
I woke
And found them true, to
My dismay.

Could you have found in me
Some fault?
I tried to hide them all from view.
But that a thing like that
Should halt
Our love! My dear! I hadn't
Thought that way of you.

You said you loved.
Could you have lied?
How hard it is for me to
Think that's so.
I shouldn't think of you at all.
I've tried
To act as if I didn't know.

But now that I've
Cried out my small lament
For all to hear, before the echoes die
My love will go the way yours went,
And I'll have better luck
Next time I try!

The Vase

The Vase pleads:

Cast me not upon the junk pile,
Deign to look at me!
Just because I don't resemble
What I used to be.

Once I was a treasured beauty,
Money deemed well spent.
Purchased on an old vacation,
Drenched in sentiment.

Once I held a place of honor
On your mantle wall.
I was instantly admired,
Seen by one and all.

Then one day a random movement,
With no ill design,
Threw me from my regal placement
Into my decline.

She answers:
It is true I dearly loved you,
Precious souvenir.
You brought back those special moments
From a bygone year.
Now your beauty days are over,
Though the memory exists.
In your current, cracked condition
You will surely not be missed.

Now to see you is no rapture,
Just life's mirror all too true.
Time brings changes unexpected
We would rather hide than view.

Collector

I don't collect what can be handled,
I don't collect what can be used.
My life is free, ungloved, unsandaled.
Life's long looks keep me amused.

While some may buy and save for keeping,
Or cherish an impromptu whim,
My memories lie in wait, just sleeping,
Waiting till I call them in.

A passing song called back a time frame,
Singing words I used to know.
Suddenly the times and place came
Showing scenes of long ago.

These are my collected treasures,
Some are happy, some are sad.
Nonetheless they give me pleasure.
Just remembering makes me glad.

Memories

A dimpled smile. A tearful look.
A broken doll. A splintered looking-glass.
A ribboned frock. A well-worn book.

'Twas just the day before I took
Her childish hand in mine. Ah! Hold it fast!
A dimpled smile. A tearful look.

The years have fled since she forsook
The artless pleasures of a little lass.
A ribboned frock. A well-worn book.

She wades no more in splashing brook,
Nor tumbles laughing gaily in the grass.
A dimpled smile, a tearful look

She still can give. The nursery nook
Is bare. My memories lie within (alas!)
A ribboned frock, a well-worn book.

Ah! Time, you are a thorough crook;
But there are things which you must pass.
A dimpled smile, a tearful look.
A ribboned frock, a well-worn book.

The Visitor

At first the tone is light and airy,
Filling in the recent past.
By the next day we are wary
For how long this phase will last.

By the third day we hear rumbles
Of the discontent within.
As the masquerading crumbles,
Tales of pain and woe begin.

This one always acts with rudeness,
Turns his back when she appears.
That one salts his speech with crudeness
And she's soon reduced to tears.

In the work world she's a loner.
No one wants to meet for lunch.
She expects that all will phone her.
No one does, and that's the crunch.

She's persistent in her trying
To establish some good friends.
But she mostly ends up crying
When the latest friendship ends.

All she wants is understanding,
Patient listening while she speaks.
She finds others too demanding,
In the company she seeks.

What she misses without knowing
Is the chance to be the star.
In its absence is the presence
Of an ever-widening scar.

Life is such a rich conundrum,
Hard to see and slow to know.
It's the old saw "give some, get some."
"What you reap is what you sow."

Our attentions seem to ease her
Frantic searching based on needs.
We do what we can to please her,
As we follow where she leads.

Gourmet Selection

There are those who always worry
About things that might occur.
Not disasters nor the tragic
But events we might prefer.

"Will I love the little new one
Just as much as sister Sue?"
"Will the roses in my garden
Grow and not obstruct my view?"

My amazement when I hear this
Never fails to turn my thought
Back to me for new assessment:
Do I think the way I ought?

Such concern for little mysteries
All encountered as we live
Seems to heighten apprehension
As a spice that life can give.

Is it that these lives are empty?
Could it be these lives are calm?
Are these "treats" to fill a vacuum,
Not a need to raise alarm?

As for me I need no seasoning.
My life's palate craves plain food.
Joy and love (in my own reasoning)
Are sufficient for my mood.

Chorus:

Oh! A life for my taste is freewheeling.
And a life filled with strife is a pill.
To the powers that be I'm appealing,
Keep my life free from strife and from ill.

Insomnia

In vain do I toss on my pillow.
(Must my blankets creep up to my knees?)
My head with equations I fill. Oh!
In vain do I toss on my pillow.
I shall weep like the wretched old willow
Are my toes doomed forever to freeze?
In vain do I toss on my pillow.
(Must my blankets creep up to my knees?)

In vain do I toss on my pillow.
(Must my blankets creep up to my knees?)
Should I pay back the money I still owe?
In vain do I toss on my pillow.
If I go to the dentist, he'll drill! Oh!
Kerchoo! There's my very first sneeze!
In vain do I toss on my pillow.
(Must my blankets creep up to my knees?)

Portrait

To look from outside in will not reveal
Tenacious chords of discontent which yearn
To disentangle memories. Born of grief
From wild encounters filled with rage and tears,
From fury mixed with fear for pain of loss.

The mismatched anguish of the early love
Now echoes through the vacant hall of time
And sends her searching vainly in the night.

Transitions

And are you less the lost for lack of tears?
Is there a spigot that has rusted on its rack?
Is there a rule that tearlessness is lack
Of love? The well is dry. The drought exists for years.

There was a time when tears ran full and wet,
Cascading in a seeming endless flow.
The pain was deep. Where is the one who knows
The cause and feels the ultimate regret?

The well is dry. The disappointed yearning buried deep.
The ache becomes a numbness of the soul.
No fueling feelings rise to make it whole.
The pain, the longing love, has gone to sleep.

The Call of Rusty Rustle

The silken rustle of her skirt
Swished on the kitchen floor.
Her high heels clacked across the room
And out the backyard door.

She called, "Goodbye!" But no one heard.
"So much for them," she thought.
She turned for one last farewell look
At what she once had sought.

Her back was straight, her footsteps firm.
She'd had her dreams of old.
But no one spoke to her of love
Her life felt bare and cold.

She'd lain awake nights hoping
Her dreams would all come true.
But time stretched on unchanging,
Her pleasures were too few.

She was alone, no more a child.
Her life was hers to live.
Inside she felt the promise
Of what she had to give.

"Go West, Young Man," said Greeley
But ladies, please stay home.
The hand that rocks the cradle
Is not supposed to roam.

The train roared in the station.
Her ticket read "one-way."
She's on her way to somewhere,
But where she could not say.

She's seeking fame and fortune,
Adventure in her breast.
Her fears remain well-hidden
While she pursues her quest.

The frontier towns are noisy.
The frontier towns are wild.
The frontier is the homeland,
For those unreconciled.

She made her way with caution.
She learned what she must learn.
She's wise beyond her years soon
With no thought to return.

She changed her name to Rustle
And rustling was her game.
She stole the hearts of many,
Which brought her wealth and fame.

The town sprang up around her.
"There's gold in them thar hills!"
She bought a little gold mine
And opened up the stills.

The town elects her mayor.
She owns it; there's no doubt.
And travelers come by thousands
To see what gold's about.

A train pulls in the station.
A face she knows descends.
She watches from her window.
She thinks, "Can I be friends?"

He needs to borrow money.
He wants to stake a claim.
He ends up on her doorstep.
He does not know her name.

The years have changed her greatly.
The blond has turned to gray.
He wants to borrow money.
He swears he will repay.

She asks about his family
And what he left behind.
He answers, "There is no one
Except a wife who's blind."

"No children, then?" she prompts him.
His hand goes to his eyes.
"Not anymore," he murmurs.
"We know not where she lies."

"She left us in the springtime,
Some twenty years ago.
We haven't heard nor seen her.
She vanished like the snow."

The woman's eyes grew thoughtful.
Her brain had formed a plan.
"I cannot lend the money
To just a single man."

"A man can be a drifter
And live a sordid life.
If you want money from me,
You must bring me your wife!"

The man's firm jaw dropped open,
"Of funding I'm bereft!"
"Here's money for the railroad."
He took the cash and left.

The train pulled in the station.
She watched them both descend.
They wait upon her doorstep.
She knows the feud must end.

They come into her chamber.
Their manner full of fear.
Their years sit heavy on them.
Her eyes begin to tear.

"Do you not know me, Mother?
Have you forgotten, Dad?
I am your long-lost daughter.
Too many years were sad."

"I had to leave your farmhouse.
Your life was not for me.
I knew that somewhere, someplace,
Was a place that I could be."

"I am now well and happy
I'm willing to forgive.
If you will say you've missed me,
We can go forth and live."

The frontier towns are noisy.
The frontier towns are wild.
The frontier towns are havens
For those unreconciled.

The message in this story
Is very plain to see.
The song her soul was singing
Was the call of destiny.

Metamorphosis

On the worn, scarred slabs of pavement,
In the city's summer street
She absorbed the skills of childhood,
How to join and then compete.

In the Springtime there was hopscotch.
There was jump rope in the fall.
Sleds and snowballs in the winter.
Sidewalk games were best of all.

"Mother, May I?" was a winner.
"Statues," "Red Light," "Bounce the Ball,"
"A, My Name Is," for the skillful
Played till dark and mother's call.

Growing up in concrete canyons.
These were pleasures without pall.
And as years rolled on relentless,
These were treasures she'd recall.

Time moves on, lifestyles evolving.
Now her children's lives bring news.
Not for them the concrete canyons;
Mountain canyons greet their views.

On a ranch in Colorado,
Spacious meadows all around
Not for miles another neighbor.
Livestock noises softly sound.

In the winter through the snow drifts,
Signs of hoof-prints on the ground.
In the Spring new life continues.
Nature's rhythm most profound.

She contrasts her own beginnings
With her grandchild's vast surround.
And, amazed, she buys a pony,
Feeling freedom newly found!

Where Did They Go?

Whatever happened to rhythm and rhyme?
Are we rejecting an old paradigm?
Poets compose reams of prose that's sublime.
Whatever happened to rhythm and rhyme?

Whatever happened to rhythm and rhyme?
Winnowing phrases to fit takes more time,
And flirting with meter is hardly a crime.
Whatever happened to rhythm and rhyme?

Whatever happened to rhythm and rhyme?
The Art of the Poem has sped past its prime.
All Blank Verse and Free Verse remind me that I'm
Missing the cadence of rhythm and rhyme,
Missing that old-fashioned rhythm and rhyme.

Friendship

We walked together, she and I
Along the winding street.
Our thoughts as much in tune as was
The rhythm of our feet.
We shared our joy, we shared our fear,
And this went on year after year.
And nothing else could interfere.
Our friendship was complete.

We walked together, she and I.
How many years have passed!
We've lived our lives and even now
The bonds of friendship last.
Some years were harsh; some years were kind.
Then time seduced her agile mind.
She left her yesterdays behind.
Now only mine stand fast.

Ruth and Naomi

I

"Entreat me not to leave thee,"
She said so long ago.
"For I must follow after
And this I surely know.
I must forsake my homeland,
My future lies with thee.
For wither thou wilt goest
Is where I, too, must be."

II

Recounting of this legend
Has never lost appeal.
Such fealty to a loved one
Surpasses our ideal.
The ease the vow was spoken
Belies the ties that bound.
The woman to her family
Before new loves were found.

III

Were her connections severed
By death, or absence spurned
Her loving ministrations
If she would have returned?
The legend doesn't tell us
The woman's private plight.
Was she, in fact, an orphan?
Did anger fuel her flight?

IV

Was there a premonition
Of events beyond her ken.
A great direct descendant
A shepherd, King of men?
Or was perhaps a widow
Restricted by her age.
Not young enough for birthing,
Too old to work for wage.

V

Where else would lie her future,
A woman on her own?
Perhaps in new surroundings,
Protected, not alone.
But with a kindly kinsman
Returning to her home,
There might be safety for her
And end the need to roam.

VI

We see through all the ages
The legend's strong appeal.
Devotion to a loved one
We all applaud with zeal.
But nowhere are we certain
What really was the case.
Whose self-interest was greater,
Whose reaction had more grace.

VII

Did the two not need each other?
Both had suffered loss and strife.
So the two went on together
In their search for a new life.

Inspiration

"Uncover your beauty,"
Said the wind to the moon
"You are veiled and I long for your gaze.
The dawn is approaching
And soon will be hiding
The shimmering light of your rays."

The moon, who was drifting
And deep in a dream,
Awoke and peeped out from a cloud.
She heard the wind's whisper.
It flattered and pleased her,
But shimmering wasn't allowed.

The wind became restless.
His ardor was high.
He didn't know quite what to do.
With clouds as her cover,
He could not see his lover.

He thought, took a deep breath, and BLEW!

New Love

The world is young today
Because I love you.
And new songs will be sung
Inside my heart.
My spirit lingers in the air
Above you.
We meet together even
Though apart.

I hear you when my dreams
Are filled with laughter.
I feel you when I have
a sense of peace.
Our souls are met
For now and ever after,
As love unites us
So shall love increase.

Wedding

Oh! The wedding!
Such a gown!
All those orchids
In her crown.
Family comes
From near and far,
Whispering wishes
With caviar.
Champagne toasts
And glasses clink.
Stacks of dishes
In the sink.
Mother's tearful,
Father's proud.
Thoughts of expenses
Not allowed.
The groom's impatient;
It's time to leave.
The bride throws kisses,
Heart's on sleeve.
Plans for months
Discharged this day.
The "Big Event"
Speeds on its way.

On the Road

Failing to find the familiar companion,
Missing the humor and pleasure of love.
Yearning to once again share common secrets,
Seeking old comfort, the treasure of love.

Keeping the memories alive on the surface,
Easily quoting a phrase from the past.
Locking the pain and the sadness inside me,
Knowing that grief and the absence would last.

Fearing the loss of the fullness of feeling,
Fearing the emptiness lying within,
What would remain when emotions erupted,
When, in the void, my true grief would begin?

Moving On

I have a fair choice.
To fathom and plumb
The depths of my soul.
To know and remove
The pain and the grief
That follow my loss
By searching within.
Recalling our love
From inside myself
And know it was good.

To move from within
And open my ears
To the music of life's
Clear melodies sung.
Some old and some new.
Some mournful refrains.
Some hauntingly sweet.
Recalling our love
From inside myself
And know it was good.

To open my eyes,
How far can I see?
What calls me to come
And leave my sad days
Asleep in my bed?
To walk with the world,
With sun and with storm.
Recalling our love
From inside myself
And know it was good.

To know in my mind
I own my whole past.
I choose what I wish
To retain and adopt,
Envelop and use.
To know I can grow.
To know that I'm strong.
Recalling our love
From inside myself
And know it was good.

Reflections and Wisdom

Life teaches wisdom.
We learn as we go.
Knowledge comes fast.
But the wisdom is slow.

Comings and Goings

"Comings" and "Goings" are landmarks of life.
They illustrate time that we've spent
On the roadway we've traveled from Birth until Death,
Shaped and molded by change and event.

We arrive on the scene through no plan of our own,
But this act becomes ours when it's done.
As the first venture out on our personal path,
It's no doubt a significant one.

There's no turning back as the road stretches out,
And the road, long and narrow, may bend.
Wherever we've journeyed, on high road or low,
We're a Traveler until the road ends.

Assessment

They came to measure it.
My new porch.
How long, how wide, how high?
I found a common theme.

How measure a life?
And by what ruler?
Inches? Feet? Yards?

What are the lengths of love
And the dimensions of
Steadfastness?

Perspective

"If Winter comes, can Spring be far Behind?"
~Percy Bysshe Shelley

I peeked around the corner in hopes that I might see
Some softly budding leaflets upon my barren tree.
But all the slender branches were naked as could be
And Spring was not yet wearing her verdant finery.

I tiptoed to the garden in the morning's early light
To catch a glimpse of color that might have bloomed at night.
But all the lovely flowers were hiding from my sight.
To bloom before Spring's entrance would not have seemed polite.

I opened up my window and heard the songbird's trill.
The sounds were bright and cheerful, although the air was chill.
"Has Spring arrived?" I questioned. The songs got strangely still.
"We do not need the Springtime for us to sing our fill."

I used to think that only the Spring would grant my dreams.
I lived for my "Tomorrows," not my "Todays," it seems.
So doing I was missing what I surely could have found
If I had only noticed the beauty all around.

"The Other Me"

I caught a glimpse reflected in a pane as I rushed by.
Who is that swollen creature with the dander in her eye?
Striding madly, headlong through the busy thoroughfare,
Intent on destination, never minding what or where.

So I caught me unaware that I was being seen.
It gave me pause to recognize "The Other Me." Between
The two of me, the one I know is gentle and sincere;
Whoever is "the other one" just needs to disappear.

Discovery

I see myself
In sharp relief.

The daily deeds and words
Worn smooth by trust and time
Are now exposed,
Left hanging there for all to see.

But mostly me.

Reverie

Rising at daybreak
Alone in the stillness.
Drinking in quiet
And vacancy's splendor.
No movements will challenge
A dreamy reflection.
No whispers intrude
On internal responses.

The passions of living
Reviewed by the author.

Sounds in Silence

In the stillness of the evening
From along the desert plain,
Breaking all the bonds of silence
Shrills the whistle of the train.

From among the summer grasses
Sometimes seen by human eye,
Sounds the love-song of the cricket
With his eager one-pitched cry.

And the squeaking of the porch swing
As it ambles to and fro,
With its steady, rusty rhythm
Binds our memories' golden glow.

We recall these sounds in silence
As they fell upon the ear.
Not because they were so different
But because they were so clear.

And their clarity confounds us
As we struggle to assess,
Did the contrast with the silence
Reinforce the sound's access?

And their presence in the absence
Of all sounds entreat the ear,
To remember both the silence,
And the contrasts that we hear.

So in life those who are missing
Though not seen are often there,
And provide us with the presence
That our souls need for repair.

Revelation

Information coming fast
To the present from the past.
Many things I used to know
Volume turned to high from low.
People, places, songs, and dates
Memory withholds, then waits.
One event recalls a chain,
Leading back in time again.

In this rear-viewed mirrored sight,
I now comprehend the flight.

Back to the Drawing Board

Salmon jump and swallows fly,
Tigers crouch and flowers die.
Every rhythm has a beat.
Every child deserves to eat.
Nature has a rule of law
Man disdains to treat with awe.
Thus the world evolves and spurns,
Greater good for sparse returns.

Temptation

"Why should the Devil get all the good tunes"*
When it takes us so long to learn scales?
It's not just the music he masters at once
He's adept as a teller of tales.

He can weave us a story of fame and of wealth
Which beckons to yearnings within,
And too soon we're enchanted and ready to join
In a plan which will lead us to sin.

He can weave us a story of pity and tears
Which he holds up for us to inspect.
And the portion which echoes so deep in our heart
Is the very one we must reject.

He's a trickster who begs us on him to rely
And we constantly fight to resist.
As we struggle to turn a deaf ear to his pleas
We gain strength in our will to persist.

*(Adapted from A. E. Stallings 1968 –)

The Question

Silently I tiptoed.
Carefully I crept.
Seeking out the moonlight
While the weary slept.
Tracing silver patterns
Scattered on the ground.
Reveling in silence
Of the vast surround.

Altered shapes confound me
Was it here I stood?
Here my vow surrendered
To lead the life I would.
From what secret cavern
Did the plan arise?
When did I envision
The road before my eyes?

"Out of step with others,"
Constantly refrained.
Sowing seeds of sorrow,
Always unexplained.
Moving on from shadow,
Turning towards the light.
Pushing thoughts behind me,
Words I couldn't fight.

Years involved in struggle,
Much of them alone.
"Out of step with others,"
As engraved in stone.
Now returning homeward.
Inner peace at last.
Completion of the circle.
Readjust the past.

Yet mystery persisted
From where the Vision came
That led to resolution
Instead of into shame.

Self-Awareness

In the land of the lame there are athletes.
In the land of the blind there is sight.
Known to all in the drum of each heartbeat
Is the soul's greatest gift and delight.

It's our dreams that inspire tomorrow
Where limits are vanquished or few.
In our courage for brave introspection
Lives the knowledge of what we can do.

The Journey

I don't believe
How far I've come
From where I came.
For now I know
I could have gone
And stayed the same.
But as I went,
From there to here
And here to there,
I grew to learn
That life held more
Than my despair.

Along the path
My eyes perceived
A distant road
That led through swamps
And rough terrain
With no abode
To call my own.
And this I spurned
To set my way
On gentler ground
With friendly folk
Who bade me stay.

Their gift to me
A chance to share
Newfound delights
Which whet my taste
And raised my eyes
To lofty heights.
My senses breathed
New precious air
And filled my ears
With magic sounds
That brought me peace
And soothed my fears.

Fear is a tool
Which we may use
To help us grow
To reach beyond
And not ignore
Our need to know.
From this evolves
A sense of self
That we can trust.
We learn to live
With strength and joy
For live we must.

Life's Wisdom

If I were to tell all the secrets I've learned
Of the best plan to follow each day,
I would say looking forward to things we enjoy
Is the happy and healthiest way.

Since no one can know what the future will bring,
At least that's what all wise men say,
Let's just live each new day while we build on the old
Refreshed by the power of play.

The beauty of play is the freedom of choice
Which provides satisfaction unbound,
And the surge of elation suffusing the soul
Is a virtue of value renowned.

For playing engages the spirit of youth
As our energy levels astound,
Which imbues us with hope for the years just ahead
Thus the power of play is profound.

Metamorphosis II

Reds and yellows, greens and blue
Timeless treasures all on view.
Crowds of colors charm my sight
Gallery grazing, my delight!

Joy arises when I see
Old friends waiting there for me.
Many are the times I've spent
Soul uplifted and content.

Awed by talent's strong embrace,
Marveling at mankind's grace.
Wandering from room to room,
Somehow banishes my gloom.

Museum visits thus include
An alteration of my mood,
(Reminding me as I depart),
That, also, is a Work of Art.

Snowtime

For Ann

Preamble

And summer left
And winter came.
For days snow fell
And fierce winds blew.
A white mist formed
That whirled and froze,
Around the forms
That marred its path.

A pristine hush prevailed when calm returned.
All marveled at the sights their eyes beheld.
Strange monolithic signs of Nature's Art,
That dazzled viewers' vision in the sun.
The most impressive measured twelve yards high.

It stood alone apart from other forms,
As if to lead a stand of nearby trees.
And day by day each person checked its height
To verify its presence still remained.
It seemed a metaphor for man's pure hope.

As weeks went by the snow began to melt,
Familiar landmarks once again appeared.
A game began to guess what lay beneath
Such artistry as winter had bestowed.
What hid inside the lone one no one knew.

The mode in winter was to walk eyes down,
Avoiding blustery winds and icy paths.
But no one left his home without the glance
In the direction of the icy shaft
To reaffirm its undiminished form.

It symbolized a strength and will to live,
Despite the knowledge of a certain death.
And people passing by recalled the times,
The challenges their own lives had survived.
And people hoped, in secret, it would last.

That winter saw a change in hearts of men.
A miracle took place inside their souls.
The beauty of the Arctic Artist's touch
Combined with wisdom that recalled their strength,
And lasted way past Springtime's gentle breath.

Inventory

I am truly three,
Myself, and I, and me.

Each of us knows why,
It's me, myself, and I.

As far as we can see,
It's I, myself, and me.

Until we're "on the shelf,"
It's me, I, and myself.

Katrina: August 23rd to 29th, 2005

Oh! The sun was bright and hot that day,
But the wind kicked up a din.
And the old men squinted eyes and said,
"Wind's different than it's been."

And the young men laughed and pruned their plants
And gave their dice a spin.
But the old ones shook their heads and said,
"A hurricane's moving in."

And the winds they blew and the storm rose up
And the folks began to fret.
"It doesn't seem it's settling down,
And everything is wet!"

A shout was heard, "The levee broke!"
"Let's go!" the young ones said.
"We'll move to higher ground in town,
Or else we'll soon be dead!"

"We'll last it out," the old ones said.
"We've done it all before."
"No, not the way the word's come down,
Get out and close the door!"

"They'll come for us," the old one said.
"It just takes some more time."
But as the hours waxed and waned,
They recognized a crime.

"They're leaving us to stay and die,"
A cry went 'round the crowd.
"What's happened to our government?
This shouldn't be allowed."

One by one the levees breached,
The walls of water surged.
Lake Pontchartrain along the East
And Mississippi merged.

Confusion reigned. No plans were made
For food or quenching thirst.
Or getting rid of human waste,
And so they did that first.

Katrina took six days to form
Until the final fall.
And orders to evacuate
Were issued last of all.

Water walls tossed homes and cars
Like toys from ground to air.
And eighty percent of New Orleans
Flooded beyond repair.

People standing on roofs waved signs.
"We need food and water," these read.
While thousands of folks clung to poles and trees,
Their hearts overflowing with dread!

The President's plane flew over,
But he never touched the ground
He looked at all below him
To see how much had drowned

He said, "Call out the Army
And help who can be found."

Thousands of soldiers and National Guards
Arrived with weapons to quell
All the rapes, thefts, and murders from rumors derived
Which denied real Disasters from Hell!

This response thwarted aid for the victims' relief
Preventing supplies to get through.
Many citizens died without shelter or care.
It seemed no one knew what to do.

Some never found a way to leave
And died before they did.
Some eighteen hundred lost their lives,
Some old, some young, some kids.

A foolhardy plan was to stack all the folks
On the seats in the Superdome stands,
And then leave them abandoned to death, rot, and waste,
An example of thoughtless commands.

News of this tragic disaster
Confounded the whole countryside.
It seemed unrealistic no plan could emerge
On a rescue that was bona fide.

Another unfortunate plan went awry
When the shipment of trailers received
Held health hazards due to formaldehyde fumes
And were not the bonanza believed.

The country opened its heart with aid
They offered food, clothing, and care.
They opened their homes to shelter these folks
Traumatized, dazed, and deep in despair.

The outrage of people brought government help
And got FEMA and Congress involved.
The picture evolved and showed rampant neglect,
The blame never could be absolved.

Now the hurricane's wreckage remains in the streets,
No earthworms inhabit this land.
Relics of homes dressed in rotten drowned wood.
There's still no one who takes full command.

"Too late we get 'schmart,'" so the old saying goes
And wisdom comes after the pain.
With knowledge comes power and hopes that the past
Will not be repeated again.

When I Am Gone

When I am gone
Remember my quick step and easy laugh.
Recall when we were youngsters, you and I.
That I was always there in your behalf.
We built our castles in the air so high
And never doubted they would reach the sky.
Please list these treasures in my epitaph
When I am gone.

When I am gone
The time will come when you relive the past
As life reveals your share of ups and downs.
If nothing else, recall that I stood fast
And met most days with grins and not with frowns.
But, most of all, the attribute that crowns,
Please know my love for you will even last
When I am gone.

Tova Sylvia Snyder Milinsky knows about "comings and goings." Born July 2, 1929, to Wolf Vladimer Snyder and Helen Eleanor Greenbaum in Philadelphia, Pennsylvani, at the age of four she moved to New York to live with her Aunt Rose and Uncle Paul Greenbaum, and younger cousin, Sandra. The following year, she moved in with her grandmother, Fanny Gibian Greenbaum, and uncles Willie, Herbert and partner Carl. Her teen years were spent with her Aunt Dorothy and her husband, Morrie Lovett. After graduating high school at the age of sixteen, she moved to Detroit where she joined her father, Wolf, and his new wife, Esther Slatkin-Ashkenazy Snyder, with her new family, seven-year-old David and new little sister, six-month-old Lee. There, Tova joined a new circle of friends, met and married Dr. Harold C. Milinsky, raised four children, earned a master's degree in social work from Wayne State University in 1966, and worked as a clinical social worker until 1993. She has five grandchildren.

Her study "Stagnation and Depression in the Elderly Group Client" was published in *Social Casework*, Mar 1987, Vol. 68(3), pages 173-179.

Tova currently lives half the year in Scottsdale, Arizona, and half the year in Beverly Hills, Michigan.

CPSIA information can be obtained at www.ICGtesting.com
Printed in the USA
LVOW12s1055050913

350721LV00004B/8/P